COMPLETE GUIDE TO DUCKLING FARMING

Expert Tips, Sustainable Practices And Efficient Care Techniques On Raising Healthy And Profitable Poultry Animals

GIOVANNI MALAKAI

© [2024] [Giovanni Malakai]. All rights reserved.

Except for brief quotations included in critical reviews and certain other noncommercial uses allowed by copyright law, no part of this publication may be reproduced, distributed, or transmitted in any form or by any means, including photocopying, recording, or other electronic or mechanical methods, without the publisher's prior written permission. Write to the publisher at the address below, addressing your letter to the "Attention: Permissions Coordinator," requesting permission.

DISCLAIMER

This book's content is solely intended for informational and educational purposes. The author and publisher of this book make no express or implied representations or warranties of any kind regarding the completeness, accuracy, reliability, suitability, or availability of the information, products, services, or related graphics contained in it, even though every effort has been made to ensure their accuracy and dependability. You consequently absolutely assume all risk associated with any reliance you may have on such material.

The author's own experiences and studies serve as the foundation for the techniques and procedures covered in this book. They might not be appropriate for every circumstance or person. Before putting any advice or recommendations from this book into practice, readers should use their own discretion and take into account their unique situation. Consulting with qualified professionals who specialize in veterinary care and animal management is always a good idea. Any direct, indirect, incidental or consequential damages resulting from using or relying on the material in this book are disclaimed by the author and publisher. Any decisions made by the reader based on the information presented herein are at their own risk.

TABLE OF CONTENTS

CHAPTER ONE 13
   INTRODUCTION TO DUCKLING FARMING 13
      KNOWING THE FUNDAMENTALS OF RAISING DUCKLINGS 13
      ADVANTAGES OF DUCK RAISING 14
      FREQUENTLY HELD MYTHS REGARDING DUCKLING FARMING 16
      ESSENTIAL TOOLS AND MATERIALS REQUIRED 17
      IMPORTANT THINGS TO THINK ABOUT BEFORE BEGINNING 19

CHAPTER TWO 21
   BEGINNING 21
      SELECTING THE APPROPRIATE DUCK BREED 21
      CREATING AN APPROPRIATE ENVIRONMENT FOR DUCKLINGS 22
      GETTING REPUTABLE DUCKLINGS 23
      PROVIDING ADEQUATE NUTRITION FOR DEVELOPMENT 25
      CREATING A MAINTENANCE AND CARE SCHEDULE 26

CHAPTER THREE 29
   INFRASTRUCTURE AND HOUSING 29
      CREATING A SECURE AND COZY DUCK COOP 29
      PROVIDING SUFFICIENT ROOM AND AIRFLOW 30
      ESTABLISHING APPROPRIATE NESTING AND BEDDING AREAS 32
      PROTECTING THE COOP FROM INTRUDERS 33
      SUSTAINING STANDARDS OF HYGIENE AND CLEANLINESS 34

CHAPTER FOUR 37
   NUTRITION AND FEEDING 37
      RECOGNIZING DUCKLINGS' NUTRITIONAL REQUIREMENTS 37

    CHOOSING THE RIGHT SUPPLEMENTS AND FEED TYPES 38

    FORMULATING A FEEDING PLAN FOR MAXIMUM GROWTH 39

    KEEPING AN EYE ON THE QUALITY AND INTAKE OF WATER 40

    TAKING CARE OF TYPICAL FEEDING PROBLEMS 42

CHAPTER FIVE 43

  MEDICAL AND VETERINARY SERVICES 43

    IDENTIFYING SYMPTOMS OF DISEASE IN DUCKLINGS 43

    PREVENTION OF FREQUENTLY OCCURRING HEALTH PROBLEMS 44

    SCHEDULES AND PROTOCOLS FOR VACCINATIONS 46

    SEEKING EXPERT ADVICE FROM A VETERINARIAN 47

    ESTABLISHING A HEALTH DOCUMENT FOR EVERY DUCKLING 48

CHAPTER SIX 51

  DEVELOPMENT AND GROWTH 51

    MONITORING DUCKLING GROWTH MILESTONES 51

    HANDLING MATURITY-RELATED HORMONAL CHANGES 52

    ENCOURAGING SOCIALIZATION AND HEALTHFUL BEHAVIORS 53

    MANAGING THE PROCESSES OF MATING AND EGG LAYING 54

    RECOGNIZING INDICATIONS OF MARKET OR BREEDING 56

CHAPTER SEVEN 57

  REPRODUCTION AND BREEDING 57

    COMPREHENDING THE DUCK BREEDING CYCLE 57

    ESTABLISHING IDEAL NESTING AND MATING CONDITIONS 58

    PROCEDURES FOR INCUBATION AND HATCHING 58

    TAKING CARE OF DUCKLINGS IN THEIR EARLY YEARS 59

    CONTROLLING HAUGHTY AND ENCOURAGING CONDUCT 60

CHAPTER EIGHT 63

PROMOTION AND DISTRIBUTION 63

FORMULATING A MARKETING PLAN FOR DUCKLING GOODS 63

FINDING TARGET MARKETS AND PREFERENCES OF CUSTOMERS 64

COMPETITIVE ANALYSIS AND PRICE STRATEGIES 65

A LOOK AT PACKAGING AND BRANDING 66

CREATING PARTNERSHIPS AND SALES CHANNELS 68

CHAPTER NINE 71

FAQS & FREQUENTLY ASKED QUESTIONS 71

ADDRESSING WORRIES ABOUT THE WELFARE OF DUCKLINGS..........71

SOLVING TYPICAL ISSUES IN DUCK FARMING 72

MANAGING CRISES AND UNFORESEEN CIRCUMSTANCES 73

FREQUENTLY ASKED QUERIES CONCERNING THE CARE OF 74

RESOURCES FOR MORE HELP AND ENCOURAGEMENT 76

CHAPTER TEN 77

ENVIRONMENTAL IMPACT AND SUSTAINABILITY 77

USING ECO-FRIENDLY METHODS IN DUCK FARMING 77

CONTROLLING WASTE AND ITS EFFECT ON THE ENVIRONMENT 78

USING ENVIRONMENTALLY FRIENDLY SOLUTIONS IN 80

ENCOURAGEMENT OF BIODIVERSITY AND NATURAL 81

ASSESSING THE LONG-TERM VIABILITY OF DUCKLING.....................83

CHAPTER ELEVEN 85

UPCOMING DEVELOPMENTS AND TRENDS 85

EXAMINING TECHNOLOGICAL DEVELOPMENTS IN DUCKLING PRODUCTION 85

TRENDS IN MARKET DEMAND AND CONSUMER PREFERENCES 86

PROSPECTS FOR GROWTH AND DIVERSIFICATION 88

CHANGING INDUSTRY AND REGULATORY STANDARDS AND HOW ...89

TECHNIQUES FOR MAINTAINING INNOVATION AND........................90

ABOUT THE BOOK

The "Complete Guide to Duckling Farming" is an all-inclusive tool created to give new and seasoned farmers alike the fundamental know-how and abilities required to be successful in duckling farming. This book explores the core ideas of duckling farming, beginning with a thorough examination of the fundamentals, including the advantages of raising ducks and busting myths about this fulfilling undertaking.

One of the most important topics discussed is choosing the appropriate breed of ducks, setting up appropriate habitats, and obtaining high-quality ducklings. It highlights the significance of a healthy diet for the best possible growth and provides a planned schedule for upkeep, so your ducklings are healthy from the start.

The book explores the needs for housing and infrastructure, offering readers advice on how to build secure and cozy duck coops, supply enough room and ventilation, and set up suitable spaces for bedding and nesting.

It also covers important topics like keeping your ducklings' environment clean and hygienic, as well as protecting them from predators.

In duckling farming, feeding, and nutrition are crucial, and this book goes into great detail about what they need to eat, how to choose the right feed and supplements, how to set up feeding schedules, and how to keep an eye on the quality and quantity of their water. It also provides advice on how to deal with typical feeding problems that farmers can run into.

Due consideration is given to health and veterinary care, including advice on identifying disease symptoms, immunization schedules, preventative measures, and the significance of seeing a veterinarian for specialist treatment. To enable proactive health management, the book places a strong emphasis on creating a health record for every duckling.

The guide offers priceless insights into monitoring development milestones, controlling hormonal shifts, encouraging healthful behaviors, and managing the breeding and reproduction processes as ducklings grow and mature. It ensures a thorough overview of the whole lifecycle by covering breeding cycles, incubation, hatching methods, and early care for ducklings.

Also covered are selling and marketing tactics, which assist farmers in creating partnerships and sales channels as well as efficient marketing plans, target market identification, and price strategies. In addition, the book answers frequently asked questions (FAQs), handles emergencies, and offers resources for more help.

The main themes include sustainability and environmental impact, with an emphasis on putting eco-friendly solutions into reality, controlling waste, promoting biodiversity, and implementing sustainable practices. In addition, the guide covers upcoming developments and advances in the duckling industry, educating farmers on technological breakthroughs, changing consumer preferences, industry regulations, and tactics for remaining creative and competitive.

CHAPTER ONE

INTRODUCTION TO DUCKLING FARMING

KNOWING THE FUNDAMENTALS OF RAISING DUCKLINGS

A gratifying business, duckling farming demands careful preparation and a basic understanding of the industry. It's important to first understand the various breeds of ducks that can be farmed. Popular breeds with distinct qualities and adaptability to different environments and uses include Pekin, Muscovy, and Khaki Campbell. It's crucial to comprehend the behavior and requirements of ducks because they are gregarious, social animals that do best in groups. They also need access to water for swimming and washing, as well as enough area to explore.

After that, familiarize yourself with duckling housing requirements. They need to be kept safe from inclement weather and predators in a secure, well-ventilated coop or pen. Providing bedding, such as wood shavings or straw, aids with comfort and cleanliness maintenance.

Since ducks are waterfowl that like splashing and foraging in water, make sure the coop has a water supply for drinking and swimming.

Duckling farming also requires careful consideration of feeding. Ducks eat a wide variety of foods, such as grains, vegetables, and commercial feeds or insects, which provide protein.

Providing a balanced diet is crucial for fostering healthy development and growth. Keep the feeding areas clean regularly to avoid infection, and keep an eye out for any symptoms of disease or malnutrition in the ducks' appetite and general health.

ADVANTAGES OF DUCK RAISING

Farmers and homesteaders find raising ducks to be an appealing alternative due to its numerous advantages. Ducks' effectiveness in controlling pests is one of their main advantages; since they naturally eat insects, snails, and other pests, fewer chemical pesticides are required.

Their nutrient-rich droppings, which enhance soil structure when handled appropriately, also add to the fertility of the soil.

Ducks lay a lot of eggs; some varieties, like the Khaki Campbell, are noted for producing large amounts of eggs. Because duck eggs are healthy and in demand for culinary applications, they give farmers an extra source of revenue. Furthermore, with the right maintenance and care, ducks are resilient and adaptable animals that can flourish in a variety of settings and climates.

Ducks can be bred for meat, eggs, feathers, and even as pets or for display, which is another advantage of growing them. Farmers may diversify their products and meet varying market demands because of this adaptability.

Furthermore, compared to other livestock, ducks require less upkeep, including minimum housing requirements and management inputs once established.

FREQUENTLY HELD MYTHS REGARDING DUCKLING FARMING

Notwithstanding the advantages, there are some widespread myths regarding raising ducklings that should be cleared up. One myth is that ducks are untidy creatures who need a lot of upkeep and cleaning. Even though they like the water and tend to make mud around water sources, ducks can be kept clean and messy by using good coop design and management techniques.

Another myth is that raising ducks is challenging or requires certain knowledge. Ducks are resilient and adaptive animals that do well with little maintenance. Suitability of housing, provision of a healthy diet, and comprehension of their requirements are essential components of a successful duckling farm.

There are however many who think that duck farming is only viable on a massive scale. Small-scale duck farming can be profitable even though scale can affect it.

This is especially true if it focuses on specialized markets like organic goods, rare breeds, or direct-to-consumer sales. Profitability and success are achievable for small-scale duck producers with effective planning, marketing, and management.

ESSENTIAL TOOLS AND MATERIALS REQUIRED

To maintain the health and productivity of your ducks, you will need certain materials and equipment when you first start duckling farming. Invest first and foremost in a proper housing structure, such as a pen or coop, that offers your ducks enough room to roam about comfortably and offers protection from the elements. To avoid respiratory problems, make sure the shelter is predator-proof and has enough ventilation.

Since water is so important to ducks, you'll need containers for drinking and swimming as well as a steady supply of water. Splashing and foraging in the water is something ducks like to do because it keeps them clean and healthy.

For children to play and swim in, think about building a pond or kid-sized swimming pools.

Feeding equipment is also necessary. Provide ducks with feeders that include grains, pellets, or mixed diets that meet their nutritional demands. Have containers available as well for veggies, greens, and protein sources such as worms or insects. To guarantee that ducks have access to fresh, well-balanced food, clean and refill feeders regularly.

Additional requirements include nesting boxes for egg-laying ducks, bedding materials (straw or wood shavings) for nesting and insulation, and basic medical supplies for normal or emergency medical care.

Before beginning duckling farming, putting these necessary supplies and equipment in place will guarantee a successful and efficient business.

IMPORTANT THINGS TO THINK ABOUT BEFORE BEGINNING

Before beginning duckling farming, there are a few important things to think about to make the endeavor successful. Determine the size and breadth of your duck business by first evaluating the space and resources that are available to you. Take into account elements like the availability of water sources, zoning laws, and the closeness of marketplaces or potential clients.

Select duck breeds that will work best for you and your surroundings. While certain varieties work well for producing eggs, others are better at producing meat or controlling pests. To make wise judgments, learn about the traits, behavior, and needs of different breeds.

Create a thorough management strategy that addresses marketing tactics, housing, food, and medical care. Make plans for unforeseen events like illness outbreaks, predator attacks, or changes in the market. To obtain knowledge and direction, think about becoming a member of regional poultry associations or consulting with seasoned duck farmers.

Finally, as you develop confidence and experience in duckling farming, start small and work your way up. Raise ducks for a variety of uses and enjoy the pleasant adventure that comes with it. Learn from your failures and accomplishments. Adjust your strategy as necessary.

CHAPTER TWO

BEGINNING

SELECTING THE APPROPRIATE DUCK BREED

Making the right breed choice when starting a duckling farming operation is essential to its success. First, think about why you are raising ducks. Breeds such as Pekin and Muscovy are well known for producing high-quality meat if raised for meat production. Indian Runner or Khaki Campbell ducks are prolific layers when it comes to egg production. Breeds like Rouen or Swedish Blue are good choices if you're looking for dual-purpose animals that are excellent producers of both meat and eggs.

Next, evaluate your resources and surroundings. Certain breeds, like the Swedish Blue, can withstand colder temperatures better than others. Some species, like the Indian Runner, do well in warmer climates. Take stock of the area you have; larger breeds can need more space than smaller ones to run around in.

Take into account the breed's disposition as well; some are more submissive and manageable, while others could be more energetic or independent.

Finally, seek advice from seasoned duck farmers or agricultural extension services. They can offer insights into regional preferences, breed appropriateness for your climate, and things to look out for in terms of potential difficulties. You can lay the groundwork for a prosperous duckling farming endeavor by carefully selecting the breed depending on your objectives, the environment, and the resources at your disposal.

CREATING AN APPROPRIATE ENVIRONMENT FOR DUCKLINGS

For ducklings to grow and thrive, it is essential to provide them with an ideal habitat. Create a duckling coop or house that has enough room for them to be comfortable and safe first. Make sure there is enough ventilation to keep the temperature at the ideal level and avoid respiratory problems, particularly in severe weather.

Use easily cleaned, absorbent materials for bedding, such as wood shavings or straws. Give broody ducks places to nest, and make sure the enclosure is safe to keep out predators. Ducks need access to water for grooming and hydration, including water sources for swimming and drinking, such as shallow ponds or water troughs.

Take into account how the habitat is arranged to encourage foraging and duckling social contact, two examples of natural activities. Provide easily accessible, well-maintained locations for feeding and watering. You may establish an environment that is beneficial to the growth and well-being of ducklings by creating a well-designed habitat that satisfies their demands for protection, shelter, and natural behaviors.

GETTING REPUTABLE DUCKLINGS

To guarantee a solid basis for your duckling farming endeavor, give quality priority while acquiring ducklings for your farm. Start by locating trustworthy hatcheries or breeders who have a track record of raising genetically sound and healthy ducklings. Seek out hatcheries that follow biosecurity protocols to reduce the possibility of disease spread.

Select ducklings whose growth rate, ability to lay eggs, or preferred meat grade are in line with your farming objectives. Upon arrival, check the ducklings for healthy indicators such as clean feathers, active movement, and awareness. Steer clear of ducklings sourced from unreliable health histories or sources with dubious hygiene standards.

Seek advice from seasoned farmers or specialists in agriculture on dependable suppliers of superior ducklings. Building a rapport with reliable vendors will help guarantee your farm has a steady supply of healthy ducklings.

Purchasing high-quality ducklings from reliable providers is a great way to start a profitable and long-lasting duckling farming business.

PROVIDING ADEQUATE NUTRITION FOR DEVELOPMENT

For ducklings to grow and develop, nutrition is essential. Give them a well-balanced meal that satisfies their needs for specific nutrients at various growth stages. Start with a beginning diet designed especially for ducklings, which will provide them with the protein, vitamins, and minerals they need to grow and develop healthily.

As the ducklings get older, gradually switch them over to grower and finisher diets, modifying the protein and vitamin levels as needed. To promote natural foraging habits and supply extra nutrients, add fresh greens, grains, and fruits to their diet. Make sure you always have access to fresh, clean water for drinking and digestion.

Regularly check on the health and progress of the ducklings, and modify their diet to their nutritional requirements and rate of growth. To encourage healthy growth and avoid nutritional deficiencies, seek advice on the best feeding practices and dietary supplements from veterinarians or experts in poultry nutrition. From hatch to maturity, you may promote healthy growth and general well-being in your ducklings by providing them with adequate nutrition.

CREATING A MAINTENANCE AND CARE SCHEDULE

Maintaining a healthy agricultural operation and providing adequate care for ducklings requires regularity and consistency. Establish a daily schedule that includes cleaning, feeding, watering, and health checks. To ensure the ducklings get the nutrition they need and stay hydrated, give them fresh feed and water frequently.

Establish a routine for cleaning the habitat, which should include clearing out dirty bedding, disinfecting water bottles, and keeping feeding places tidy. Regularly check on the health of your family to look for any indications of disease or injury. Address any concerns right once to stop the spread of illness and maintain good health.

Create procedures for biosecurity, emergency response plans, and predator avoidance to protect your farm's infrastructure and ducklings. Maintain thorough records of all treatments, health observations, and feeding plans to monitor development and spot trends or possible issues.

Consult veterinary specialists or agricultural specialists for regular health examinations, immunizations, and advice on how to prevent illnesses. You can ensure the sustainability of your farming operation and improve the productivity and well-being of your ducklings by creating and following a thorough care and maintenance schedule.

CHAPTER THREE

INFRASTRUCTURE AND HOUSING

CREATING A SECURE AND COZY DUCK COOP

For the sake of your ducks, you must build a secure and cozy coop. To begin with, plan a coop that gives your ducks plenty of room to go about. As a general guideline, give each duck at least 4 square feet of area. To maintain adequate air circulation and avoid moisture buildup, which can cause respiratory problems in ducks, the coop must also have adequate ventilation.

You should consider the materials when designing the coop. Select weather-resistant and long-lasting materials that can tolerate a range of weather circumstances. Make sure the coop has a sturdy roof to shield your ducks from the sun and weather. Install windows or vents as well to provide fresh air into the coop.

Provide comfortable locations in the coop for ducks to lay their eggs for nesting. To create comfortable nesting areas, use straw or other appropriate bedding materials.

To avoid overpopulation and guarantee that every duck has a spot to lay eggs without interference, provide an adequate number of nesting boxes according to the number of ducks you have.

Finally, add elements that render the coop impervious to predators. To keep predators from accessing the ducks, block openings with strong wire mesh and lock the coop. Check the coop frequently for indications of damage or vulnerable areas that might be used by predators.

PROVIDING SUFFICIENT ROOM AND AIRFLOW

Enough space and ventilation in the coop are essential for duck husbandry. Ducks need room to roam around and carry out their natural activities, which include swimming and foraging. Make sure each duck in the coop has at least 4 square feet of space so they can move around comfortably.

Maintaining a high standard of air quality inside the coop requires proper ventilation.

Strategically place windows or vents to let in fresh air and prevent the accumulation of moisture and ammonia from duck droppings. In addition to regulating humidity and temperature, good ventilation helps provide a healthy habitat for your ducks.

Take into account the coop's design to make the most use of available space. To increase extra floor space and give ducks places to rest or perch, use ramps or raised platforms. Steer clear of overpopulation, which can cause stress, hostility, and health problems in ducks. To keep things clean and stop odors from building, regularly wash and discard dirty bedding.

Regularly check the coop's temperature and humidity levels, especially in the event of severe weather. As necessary, make adjustments to guarantee the comfort and well-being of your ducks. Encouraging the health of your flock and successfully farming ducks depends on providing enough room and ventilation.

ESTABLISHING APPROPRIATE NESTING AND BEDDING AREAS

It's critical to create appropriate nesting and bedding facilities for your ducks' comfort and well-being. Select absorbent bedding materials like wood shavings, shredded paper, or straw. Cover the floor of the coop with a thick layer of bedding to act as a cushion and absorb moisture from the droppings of the ducks.

Within the coop, set aside particular spaces for laying eggs. Give ducks places to lay their eggs, such as nesting boxes or quiet areas with cozy bedding. To entice ducks to use the nesting locations for depositing their eggs, make sure they are quiet and unoccupied.

Maintain the coop's hygiene and cleanliness by routinely inspecting and replacing any filthy bedding. Your ducks may develop health issues as a result of bacteria and parasites that are harbored in dirty bedding. To avoid infection, keep the spaces around the nests clean and take out any cracked or unclean eggs at once.

Regularly check the bedding's condition and replace it as necessary. Bedding can be rearranged by ducks to suit their tastes, so make the necessary adjustments to provide them with cozy and welcoming nesting areas. Your ducks will live in a healthy and stress-free environment if they have adequate bedding and nesting places.

PROTECTING THE COOP FROM INTRUDERS

One of the most important parts of duck farming is keeping your ducks safe from harm. By putting in place strong security measures, you can protect your flock and avoid losses brought on by predators. To start, secure the coop's perimeter from foxes, raccoons, and other predators by using wire mesh or a strong fence.

Regularly check the coop for any openings, cracks, or vulnerable areas that a predator might use. To stop unwanted access, these places should be reinforced or repaired as a way. Put predator-proof locks on windows and doors to make it difficult for intruders to open them.

To keep predators away from the coop, think about utilizing deterrents such as predator decoys, motion-activated lights, or sound alarms. To make the coop perimeter unfriendly to potential intruders, use these deterrents in appropriate locations.

Teach your ducks to react and identify danger cues, including strange noises or alarm calls. When predators are close by, this can assist them in hiding or finding safety. You can guarantee your ducks' safety and drastically lower the chance of predation by putting in place a multi-layered security system.

SUSTAINING STANDARDS OF HYGIENE AND CLEANLINESS

It is imperative to uphold hygienic and sanitary standards in the duck coop to avert disease outbreaks and foster the well-being of your flock.

Create a routine cleaning program to clean the coop floor and nesting areas of dirtied bedding, droppings, and debris.

Soiled bedding should be picked up and disposed of appropriately using a shovel or rake. To keep the coop dry and odor-free, replace the bedding with new, clean material.

To get rid of bacteria and parasites, clean and sanitize surfaces, nest boxes, and feeding/watering locations regularly.

Make sure the coop is well drained to avoid standing water, which invites pests and exacerbates moisture-related problems. To encourage air circulation and avoid humidity buildup, use absorbent materials in damp places and make sure there is enough ventilation.

Keep a close eye on your ducks' health and look out for any symptoms of disease or infection. To stop illness from spreading across the flock, isolate any sick or injured ducks.

Put biosecurity precautions in place to lessen the chance of exposing your ducks to infections. These include restricting outside visitors and managing the flow of supplies and equipment.

You can give your ducks a clean, hygienic habitat that reduces the risk of illness and ensures their well-being by upholding strict cleaning and hygiene standards. Successful duck husbandry requires a strict regimen of sanitation and cleaning.

CHAPTER FOUR

NUTRITION AND FEEDING

RECOGNIZING DUCKLINGS' NUTRITIONAL REQUIREMENTS

Particular dietary needs are essential to the growth and development of ducklings. They need a diet that is well-balanced and high in carbohydrates, proteins, vitamins, and minerals. Vitamins and minerals promote general health and immunity, whereas proteins are necessary for the growth of muscle and tissue. They get energy from carbohydrates for their daily tasks. For ducklings to grow healthily, it is essential to comprehend these dietary requirements.

When organizing their nutrition, take into account duckling-specific beginning feeds. Higher protein content in these diets helps to assist early-stage fast growth. Incorporate supplements such as calcium and vitamin D for general health and bone formation. Enhancing their nutritional intake can also be accomplished by offering a varied diet that includes a variety of grains, veggies, and protein sources like mealworms or insects.

As they get older, their nutrition can be adjusted with the assistance of a veterinarian and regular growth assessments. When they approach adolescence, adjustments can include switching to grower diets with a little lower protein level. You may lay a solid basis for their development and well-being by recognizing and addressing their dietary needs at an early age.

CHOOSING THE RIGHT SUPPLEMENTS AND FEED TYPES

For ducklings to grow and thrive to their full potential, it is essential to select the correct meal varieties and supplements. To begin, use premium starter feed made especially for ducklings.

Their fast growth and development are supported by the nutritional balance of these meals. For general health, look for feeds that provide sufficient amounts of protein and important vitamins and minerals.

Supplements are essential for improving their diet. To promote bone development and avoid inadequacies, think about incorporating calcium supplements. Supplemental vitamins, particularly vitamin D, are critical for the health and function of their immune systems. Probiotics can also help with good digestion and nutrient absorption when added to food.

When choosing feed, use pellets or crumbles that are appropriate for the small beaks and digestive tracts of ducklings. Steer clear of adult duck meals, as they might not provide the nutrients growing ducklings need. To make sure their feed stays balanced and suitable for their stage of growth, regularly evaluate their physical condition and seek advice from a poultry nutritionist.

FORMULATING A FEEDING PLAN FOR MAXIMUM GROWTH

Setting up a feeding regimen is essential to guaranteeing ducklings the best possible development and growth. First, feed them often throughout the day, especially in the first several weeks. Several times a day, provide modest amounts of beginning meals to satisfy their high energy needs for growth.

As the ducklings grow older, progressively decrease the number of feedings each day while increasing the quantity. Keep an eye on their eating patterns and modify the feeding plan by their growth rate and hunger. Always have fresh water available to avoid dehydration, particularly in hot conditions.

As they get older, think about adding delights like chopped fruits or vegetables and greens to their diet. Their meals are more varied and nutrient-rich thanks to these additions. Make sure they are getting enough nutrients for healthy growth by routinely cleaning the feeding apparatus and keeping an eye on feed consumption.

KEEPING AN EYE ON THE QUALITY AND INTAKE OF WATER

Water is vital to the health and welfare of ducklings. In particular, during warmer months or times of greater activity, keep a careful eye on their water consumption to make sure they stay hydrated. Give them easily accessible shallow containers filled with fresh, clean water.

Make sure the water quality is regularly checked to make sure pollutants and algae development are not present. To stop bacteria from growing, replace water containers every day and give them a thorough cleaning. Steer clear of water sources that might be contaminated or contain substances that are toxic to ducklings.

Placing water bottles close to their feeding area and making sure they can easily get them will encourage regular drinking. Keep an eye out for symptoms of dehydration in them, such as decreased appetite or lethargy.

Resolve any problems with the water quality as soon as possible to keep the ducklings as healthy and hydrated as possible.

TAKING CARE OF TYPICAL FEEDING PROBLEMS

When feeding ducklings, it's important to deal with frequent problems that could come up. Overfeeding is a prevalent issue that can result in obesity and other health issues. To avoid overfeeding, keep an eye on how much food they are consuming and modify portion sizes accordingly.

Inadequate nutrition is another problem, which can arise from providing poor-quality or unsuitable meals. Make sure you offer premium beginning foods that are tailored to the dietary requirements of ducklings. Add supplements as necessary to make up for any gaps.

Keep an eye out for symptoms of digestive troubles, such as bloating or diarrhea, as these could point to nutritional deficiencies or infections. See a veterinarian if you observe any strange feeding-related symptoms or behaviors. Your ducklings' health and well-being as they develop can be guaranteed by taking quick action to solve these typical feeding problems.

CHAPTER FIVE

MEDICAL AND VETERINARY SERVICES

IDENTIFYING SYMPTOMS OF DISEASE IN DUCKLINGS

As with other things, the ability to spot illness in ducklings early on and respond quickly is essential. A primary indicator to be aware of is alterations in conduct or degree of activity. A duckling may show early signs of disease if it suddenly becomes listless, shows no interest in feeding, or withdraws from the flock. Furthermore, be alert to any physical anomalies, such as odd swelling, drooping wings, or discolored feathers.

The ducklings' excrement is something else to keep an eye on. Any noticeable variations in the frequency, color, or consistency of feces may indicate illnesses or digestive problems.

Red flags include respiratory symptoms such as coughing, sneezing, or nasal discharge that should not be disregarded. When a duckling shows symptoms of sickness, it's critical to act quickly to stop the disease from spreading and make sure it gets the treatment it needs.

Finally, pay close attention to the flock's general health. If several ducklings show the same symptoms, it could be a sign of a communicable illness that has to be treated right away. Frequent health examinations and familiarity with typical behavior can assist you in identifying sickness early on, enabling prompt intervention and improved results for your ducklings.

PREVENTION OF FREQUENTLY OCCURRING HEALTH PROBLEMS

Preventive actions are essential for preserving duckling health and welfare. Making sure the living space is tidy and sanitary is one of the first tasks. Maintain a regular cleaning schedule for the duckling's living space, including the bedding, waterers, and feeders, to avoid the growth of infections and bacteria that could be harmful to their health.

Another important component in avoiding frequent health problems is proper nutrition. Give ducklings a well-balanced meal consisting of clean water, fresh greens, and commercial feed.

Food that is stale or infected should not be given to children as this might cause nutrient shortages and stomach problems.

It is imperative to have biosecurity measures in place to stop the entry and spread of pathogens. To lower the danger of illness transmission, confine new ducklings before exposing them to the current flock and restrict visitor numbers. To reduce contamination, clean footwear, and equipment regularly.

You can considerably lower the chance of common health problems in your ducklings by being proactive and implementing measures like keeping them clean, feeding them well, and using biosecurity. This will ensure that they flourish and mature into healthy adults.

SCHEDULES AND PROTOCOLS FOR VACCINATIONS

A vital component of raising ducklings is vaccination, which guards against frequent illnesses and guarantees a healthy flock. Effective disease prevention requires knowledge of immunization schedules and practices. To create a vaccination schedule that is unique to your ducklings and takes into account local illness risks, speak with a veterinarian.

Duck hepatitis, avian influenza, and duck viral enteritis (DVE) are among the common vaccines given to ducklings. Typically, vaccination programs begin in the first few weeks of life for ducklings, and booster doses may be necessary to preserve immunity. Adhere to your veterinarian's suggested vaccination schedule and dosage.

Maintaining vaccination efficacy also depends on handling and storage procedures that are appropriate. Vaccines should be kept at the specified temperature; exposure to strong sunlight or extremely high or low temperatures may reduce their efficacy.

To avoid contamination and guarantee that the vaccine reaches its intended recipients, administer vaccinations using sterile equipment and procedures.

Review and change your immunization schedule regularly to reflect evolving health concerns or shifting disease threats. You may greatly lower the chance of illness outbreaks and protect your ducklings' health by being vigilant about immunizations and following advised schedules.

SEEKING EXPERT ADVICE FROM A VETERINARIAN

For duckling health, basic maintenance and preventative measures are crucial, but occasionally, seeking expert care from a veterinarian becomes necessary.

In addition to performing health examinations and offering professional advice on housing, diet, and disease-preventive techniques, veterinarians are essential in the diagnosis and treatment of ailments.

Choose a veterinarian who specializes in poultry or avian medicine when choosing one for your ducklings. Plan routine examinations and consultations to keep an eye on the flock's health and quickly handle any new problems that may arise. Additionally, veterinarians can offer advice on nutritional supplements, general flock management techniques, and parasite control.

Seek veterinary care as soon as possible in cases of disease or injury to guarantee prompt diagnosis and treatment. To aid sick or injured ducklings in recovering, veterinarians can conduct diagnostic tests, provide prescriptions for drugs, and provide supportive care. Building a solid rapport with a reliable veterinarian is crucial to ensuring your ducklings' health and welfare at all growth phases.

ESTABLISHING A HEALTH DOCUMENT FOR EVERY DUCKLING

To effectively manage and monitor the health status of each duckling, it is imperative to maintain correct health records.

Information including breed, date of birth, immunization history, weight measurements, and any noteworthy medical observations or treatments should all be included in a thorough health record.

Start by keeping a distinct health record, with easy-to-update and easily accessible information, for every duckling. Add tags or other identifying markers to help you identify individual ducklings and monitor their development over time. Keep track of all veterinary consultations, prescriptions filled, and health examinations performed.

Update the medical records regularly with new details, such as immunization dates, developmental milestones, and any modifications to the patient's condition. This facilitates trend tracking, early detection of possible health issues, and well-informed flock management choices.

During consultations, provide your veterinarian with pertinent health information so they can provide recommendations for individualized care.

You may track a duckling's growth and development, keep an eye out for any health problems, and make sure they receive the right care throughout their life cycle by keeping thorough health records for each one. Maintaining accurate records is essential to maximizing the well-being and output of your duckling farm.

CHAPTER SIX

DEVELOPMENT AND GROWTH

MONITORING DUCKLING GROWTH MILESTONES

Ducklings are amazing to watch grow from the time they hatch. They are sensitive at first and need a cozy, secure space to grow. It's essential to monitor their developmental milestones to make sure they continue to develop and stay healthy. Ducklings begin to develop feathers and gain mobility at about one week of age. You must feed them at this period to ensure their growth is at its best.

Ducklings begin to explore more actively and form social behaviors when they are two to three weeks old. They are starting to engage with their surroundings and other ducklings during this thrilling phase.

 Their physical and mental growth is aided by providing a stimulating habitat with access to water for swimming and foraging opportunities.

Ducklings should exhibit adult-like habits and have a fully developed feather coat by the time they are four to six weeks old. At this point, tracking their development entails evaluating their weight increase, general health, and preparedness for switching to a more diversified diet. See a veterinarian regularly to make sure they are meeting their growth milestones as planned.

HANDLING MATURITY-RELATED HORMONAL CHANGES

Ducklings have major hormonal changes as they become adults, which affect their behavior and ability to reproduce. A healthy and peaceful duckling farm depends on recognizing and adjusting to these changes. Ducks achieve sexual maturity at about six months of age, and hormonal changes can cause aggressive behavior, particularly in the male population.

Giving ducks enough room and resources to express their normal activities without endangering the environment or one another is part of managing hormonal changes in ducks.

Keeping men and females apart during mating seasons helps lessen hostility and guarantee productive reproduction. Positively channeling hormonal energy can also be achieved by offering rewarding activities like social interactions and foraging chances.

Farmers can identify any odd behaviors or symptoms of suffering associated with hormone shifts by regularly observing and interacting with ducks. By modifying the diet, surroundings, and social interactions in light of these findings, a duckling farm can remain well-balanced and healthy.

ENCOURAGING SOCIALIZATION AND HEALTHFUL BEHAVIORS

Ducklings need to be socialized and encouraged to engage in appropriate behaviors for their general development and well-being. Early exposure to water promotes natural behaviors in ducklings, like as swimming and foraging, which are essential for their mental and physical development.

They learn social cues and flock hierarchy through socialization with other ducklings and adult ducks.

Healthy habits like exercise and instinctive foraging are encouraged when there is enough room for movement and discovery in a secure and stimulating setting. Ducks flourish in settings that allow them to freely engage in their natural habits, which lowers stress levels and improves their general health.

The relationship between ducks and farmers can be strengthened and positive behaviors can be encouraged through regular handling and gentle training sessions with ducklings. Establishing regular feeding, exercise, and socialization schedules helps to maintain a population of healthy, well-behaved ducklings.

MANAGING THE PROCESSES OF MATING AND EGG LAYING

On a duckling farm, managing the mating and egg-laying procedures calls for meticulous preparation and oversight. Since ducks lay a lot of eggs, it is crucial to provide them with appropriate nesting places with cozy bedding and seclusion to maximize egg production. Ducks' health and reproductive condition can be evaluated by keeping an eye on the quantity and quality of their eggs.

The goal of managing mating is to keep the ratio of males to females balanced to keep ducks from overmating and becoming stressed. Successful reproduction is supported by giving them access to clean water, and enough food, and avoiding environmental disturbances during mating seasons. Proper egg collection and storage guarantees freshness and viability for hatching or ingestion.

Farmers can stay informed about the reproductive health of their duck population through routine nesting area inspections, egg collecting, and mating behavior monitoring. Using techniques to encourage instinctive egg-laying and natural mating behaviors is part of what makes a duckling farm productive and sustainable.

RECOGNIZING INDICATIONS OF MARKET OR BREEDING READINESS

One of the most important aspects of effectively running a duckling farm is recognizing indications of market or breeding readiness. Achieving the ideal weight and size indicators by breed standards is crucial for ducks meant for the market. Ducks' market readiness is assessed by tracking growth rates, feed conversion efficiency, and general health metrics.

Evaluating the reproductive health and maturity of ducks is crucial for breeding purposes. Ducks are ready to reproduce when they exhibit behaviors related to mating, consistent egg production, and physical preparedness. Breeding ducks are kept in the best possible condition for successful reproduction and high-quality offspring through the completion of health tests and genetic evaluations.

Reliability in record-keeping and data analysis helps monitor ducks' preparedness for the market or breeding.

CHAPTER SEVEN

REPRODUCTION AND BREEDING

COMPREHENDING THE DUCK BREEDING CYCLE

It's important to comprehend the ducks' normal reproductive cycle when breeding them. During the spring and summer, when daylight increases and hormones are released, ducks pair to promote reproductive behavior. The competitive behavior of male ducks, referred to as drakes, for females, is called courting. This can include vocalizations, physical contact, and displays of plumage.

A female will start laying eggs in an isolated nest as soon as she and a male successfully mate. Ducks are renowned for their sly nesting practices; they frequently select safe havens near bodies of water. Until she develops a clutch, which can include anywhere from a few to several dozen eggs depending on the species, the female will lay one egg every day.

ESTABLISHING IDEAL NESTING AND MATING CONDITIONS

Duck farmers need to create ideal conditions for successful mating and nesting. This involves making sure the ducks have enough room to go around and socialize without feeling crowded, as stress can impede the success of reproduction. In addition, keeping breeding ducks healthy and fertile requires feeding them a well-balanced diet high in nutrients.

Establishing appropriate nesting sites is crucial. This entails creating nesting boxes or shelters that are filled with hay or straw for soft bedding, imitating the natural setting in which ducks would normally construct their nests. To reduce disruptions that could interfere with the breeding process, the nesting place should be remote, peaceful, and protected from predators.

PROCEDURES FOR INCUBATION AND HATCHING

After the eggs are laid, they need to be properly incubated for them to grow and hatch.

Alternatively, duck farmers can let the mother duck naturally incubate the eggs. Artificial incubators are also an option. Artificial incubators offer fine-grained regulation of both temperature and humidity, guaranteeing ideal circumstances for the development of embryos.

To avoid uneven heating and support good embryo growth, it is crucial to often check on and rotate the eggs during incubation. Ducklings begin to hatch approximately 28 days after they are placed in the incubator. It can take several hours to complete this procedure, therefore it's imperative to avoid stressing or hurting the ducklings or the eggs during this period.

TAKING CARE OF DUCKLINGS IN THEIR EARLY YEARS

Ducklings need to be given care and attention as soon as they hatch to survive. Since baby ducklings are susceptible to chilly temperatures, it is imperative to provide them with a warm and dry habitat.

A brooder equipped with a heated pad or light can produce a comfortable environment for ducklings to flourish.

For ducklings to grow and develop healthily, it is essential to feed them a specific beginning feed that is tailored to meet their nutritional requirements. The higher protein content is usually seen in this meal, which helps with the early life stages of rapid growth. Furthermore, it's critical to provide clean water for swimming and drinking (if at all feasible) to support natural behavior and hydration.

CONTROLLING HAUGHTY AND ENCOURAGING CONDUCT

The term "brooding" describes the protective nurturing that mother ducks give to their ducklings. This entails providing them with warmth, teaching them how to find food on their own, and shielding them from harm. It is the responsibility of duck farmers to protect the mother and her ducklings while also observing and encouraging their natural brooding patterns.

When a mother duck is unable to provide for her ducklings or when there are orphaned ducklings in need of parental care, foster care may be required. Fostering is placing ducklings with a broody hen or another duck that will act as a surrogate mother and provide them the attention and direction they need to grow.

Duck farmers can guarantee the long-term viability of their operations and effectively raise healthy ducklings by comprehending and putting into practice the right breeding, nesting, incubation, and care practices.

CHAPTER EIGHT

PROMOTION AND DISTRIBUTION

FORMULATING A MARKETING PLAN FOR DUCKLING GOODS

It's critical to begin developing a marketing plan for your products with a solid grasp of your product and its distinctive selling features. Start by determining the salient characteristics of your duckling items that distinguish them from rival offerings. This could involve elements like exceptional quality, distinctive flavor characteristics, or organic farming practices. You may adjust your marketing messaging to emphasize these features and appeal to your target demographic once you have a firm understanding of what makes your items unique.

Next, think about the different marketing platforms you might use to successfully reach your target demographic. This could use conventional channels like print advertising and farmer's markets, as well as digital platforms like social media, email marketing, and e-commerce websites. Selecting the channels that best fit the tastes and behaviors of your target market is crucial because each one has advantages and target demographics of its own.

Finally, remember to consistently monitor and assess the outcomes of your marketing initiatives. To enhance your marketing approach over time, use data analytics tools to track campaign performance, pinpoint areas for development, and make data-driven decisions.

FINDING TARGET MARKETS AND PREFERENCES OF CUSTOMERS

The secret to a successful duckling farming enterprise is having a thorough understanding of your target market's tastes. To find possible client categories based on characteristics like behavior patterns, psychographics, and demographics, start by performing market research. Using this data, you can design thorough buyer personas that serve as representations of your ideal clients and serve as a roadmap for your product development and marketing initiatives.

After determining which consumers to target, learn more about their wants and preferences for duckling products. This could involve things like favorite meat pieces, cooking techniques, favored flavors, and preferred packaging. You can adjust your product offers and marketing messaging to appeal to your target audience and increase sales by being aware of these subtleties.

Remember that consumer tastes can change over time, therefore it's critical to remain adaptable and aware of market developments. Engage with your clients regularly via social media, feedback forms, and surveys to get their ideas and modify your plans.

COMPETITIVE ANALYSIS AND PRICE STRATEGIES

Choosing the appropriate price plan is essential to the success of your duckling farming enterprise. To comprehend the pricing environment in your industry, start by performing a competition analysis. Determine the main rivals and examine their value propositions, product lines, and price policies. By using this information, you can ensure that your duckling goods offer clients a distinct value while positioning them in a competitive market.

Think about things like production costs, market demand, perceived value, and pricing elasticity while formulating your pricing plan. Strike a balance between affordability and profitability to draw in clients and increase sales. To increase sales and take market share, you might also investigate price strategies including bundle pricing, promotional pricing, and dynamic pricing.

To gradually improve your price plan, keep an eye on the state of the market, the activities of your competitors, and consumer feedback. To keep ahead of the competition and optimize your pricing strategy, do pricing experiments and evaluate the outcomes.

A LOOK AT PACKAGING AND BRANDING

Branding and packaging are essential for drawing in clients and setting your products apart from those of your rivals. Create visually arresting and informative packaging that highlights the superior quality and distinctiveness of your items first. To promote your brand values and appeal to environmentally conscious consumers, use eco-friendly materials, vivid graphics, and clear product information.

When crafting your brand identity, concentrate on telling an engaging story that appeals to your intended market. This could be showcasing the history of your farm, the use of sustainable agricultural methods, or your dedication to animal care. To increase brand awareness and customer loyalty, consistently reinforce your brand messaging on all touchpoints, such as online platforms, marketing materials, and packaging.

To remain current and competitive in the market, assess and change your branding and packaging tactics regularly. To sustain a strong brand presence and increase sales, get input from clients and industry experts, keep an eye on consumer preferences and packaging design trends, and modify your strategy as necessary.

CREATING PARTNERSHIPS AND SALES CHANNELS

Reaching your target audience and optimizing sales prospects for your duckling products depends on selecting the appropriate sales channels and alliances. Assess the several sales channels that are accessible, including retail distribution, internet marketplaces, direct-to-consumer sales, and collaborations with food service providers.

Think about things like cost-effectiveness, reach, and compatibility with the purchasing habits of your target market.

If you decide against direct sales, invest in social media marketing, e-commerce platforms, and search engine optimization (SEO) to establish a powerful online presence. Make a compelling website that highlights your goods, narrates the history of your company, and facilitates orders and client contact.

Find possible retail partners for your retail distribution who share the same values as your target market and brand. To increase your reach and gain access to new client groups, cultivate ties with farmers' markets, specialized food stores, and supermarket stores. Work together to produce duckling items for commercial usage with food service providers, such as restaurants, caterers, and institutional customers.

Optimize your sales strategy and promote long-term growth and success for your duckling farming business by regularly assessing the effectiveness of your partnerships and sales channels, monitoring sales KPIs, and asking for input from partners and customers.

CHAPTER NINE

FAQS & FREQUENTLY ASKED QUESTIONS

ADDRESSING WORRIES ABOUT THE WELFARE OF DUCKLINGS

Successful duck farming depends on protecting the welfare of the ducklings. A common worry is having enough beds and shelter. Even in their early days, ducklings require a warm, dry, and draft-free habitat. It is best to use a brooder box or enclosure with appropriate bedding, like wood shavings or straw. Regularly checking the temperature and humidity levels is essential to avoiding health concerns including respiratory disorders.

Nutrition is another essential component. For healthy growth and development, ducklings need a well-balanced diet high in protein and other necessary components. The best-starting meal for ducklings is commercially available, but for extra nourishment, you may also add greens and insects. To avoid pollution and illnesses, there should always be access to fresh, clean water, and water needs to be maintained in good condition.

Finally, handling and socializing are critical to the welfare of ducklings. Being gregarious creatures, they gain by interacting with people and other ducklings. Careful handling eases their anxiety and reduces stress as they get used to the human touch. Enrichment, such as swimming in shallow water pools, encourages their natural behaviors and overall well-being.

SOLVING TYPICAL ISSUES IN DUCK FARMING

Numerous typical issues can emerge in duck farming, but they can be handled with the right information and preemptive action. The purity and quality of the water is one problem. Fresh, clean water is necessary for ducks to bathe and drink. To stop bacterial growth and illnesses, clean waterers frequently and replace the water. Keeping an eye on water quality metrics like pH and chlorine levels is crucial to preserving the environment's health.

Predator attacks are another prevalent issue. Predators such as foxes, raccoons, and birds of prey can harm ducks. Predators can be discouraged by the use of guard animals like dogs, predator-proof houses, and secure fencing. The danger of nighttime attacks can be decreased by putting security measures in place, such as keeping ducks in a locked coop.

Health problems in duck husbandry include respiratory diseases and parasites. Preventing and managing these issues can be achieved by immunization campaigns, routine health examinations, and good cleanliness habits. It is advised to consult a veterinarian to properly diagnose and treat medical conditions.

MANAGING CRISES AND UNFORESEEN CIRCUMSTANCES

In duck husbandry, unforeseen circumstances and emergencies can arise, necessitating prompt and decisive response. Severe weather, such as storms or intense heat, is one frequent emergency. To shield ducks from inclement weather, give them cover and shade and make sure they have access to fresh water and ventilation. In the event of severe weather, installing a backup power source for heating or cooling equipment is advised.

Epidemics are another dangerous scenario. Put afflicted ducks in quarantine, follow stringent biosecurity protocols, and seek veterinary advice for diagnosis and treatment. Keeping surfaces, tools, and equipment clean aids in halting the spread of illness in duck colonies.

Accidents or injuries that happen by mistake, like ducklings getting hurt or trapped, also need to be attended to very quickly. Maintain a first aid box stocked with necessary items, and tend to wounds right away to avoid infection and worsening of the situation.

FREQUENTLY ASKED QUERIES CONCERNING THE CARE OF DUCKLINGS

Answering these frequently asked questions (FAQs) will help beginners better understand and care for their ducklings. Diets and feeding schedules are among the often-asked questions.

From the moment of hatching, ducklings should have access to beginning feed, which should be freely available. As they get older, gradually introduce greens and other nutrients according to suggested dietary standards.

Inquiries concerning housing needs are also frequent. Ducklings require a well-ventilated, safe, dry, and warm habitat. It's ideal to use a brooder box or pen with bedding made of wood shavings or straw. Make sure there is enough room for each duckling to avoid crowding and encourage healthy development.

Duckling well-being and health are also popular subjects. To avoid illness and keep your health at its best, be immunized against diseases, and practice good cleanliness. Novices should keep an eye out for symptoms of disease in their ducklings' behavior, appetite, and droppings, and seek veterinarian assistance when necessary. Providing toys and shallow water pools as enrichment also helps with their development and well-being.

RESOURCES FOR MORE HELP AND ENCOURAGEMENT

Having access to resources for further help and support is essential for novice duck farmers to succeed. Universities and local agricultural extension agencies frequently provide training courses, workshops, and instructional materials on duck farming techniques. These sources offer helpful information on a variety of subjects, including health management, housing, nutrition, and biosecurity precautions.

You can also acquire guidance and recommendations from seasoned duck farmers by participating in online forums and communities. Beginners can learn from others in the duck farming community by asking questions, sharing experiences, and participating in social media groups or specialized forums. Making connections with other farmers can provide important insights and support systems.

Furthermore, comprehensive information on diverse facets of duck farming can be found in books, articles online, and agricultural periodicals.

CHAPTER TEN

ENVIRONMENTAL IMPACT AND SUSTAINABILITY

USING ECO-FRIENDLY METHODS IN DUCK FARMING

To raise ducks sustainably, methods must be adopted that limit adverse effects on the environment while retaining high productivity. Optimizing land use is essential for preventing habitat degradation and protecting natural resources. This can be accomplished by using appropriate land management practices, such as rotational grazing, in which ducks are routinely relocated to avoid overgrazing and soil erosion. Furthermore, adding agroforestry techniques to the farm by planting trees and bushes can strengthen the fertility of the soil, give waterfowl shade, and increase biodiversity.

Responsibly managing water resources is another essential element of sustainable duck farming. Reducing water waste and ensuring sustainable water usage can be achieved by putting into practice water conservation techniques including drip irrigation systems, rainwater collection, and effective watering schedules. By supporting aquatic biodiversity and serving as a habitat for other species, using natural water bodies like ponds or wetlands on the farm can also improve environmental balance.

Moreover, animal welfare and health must be given priority in sustainable duck farming. This entails giving ducks a natural, stress-free habitat, cutting back on the usage of pesticides and antibiotics, and switching to organic feed methods. Farmers may help create a more ethical and sustainable method of duck farming by supporting the health of the birds and abstaining from toxic substances.

CONTROLLING WASTE AND ITS EFFECT ON THE ENVIRONMENT

Reducing the negative effects of duck farming on the environment requires efficient waste management. By putting waste management techniques into practice, such as composting bedding materials and duck dung, organic waste can be converted into nutrient-rich soil amendments that minimize greenhouse gas emissions and the need for synthetic fertilizers. Composting systems that are run correctly also aid in odor management and help shield water from contaminants.

Water quality and ecosystems must be safeguarded by managing organic waste as well as runoff and erosion from duck farming activities. Soil erosion and water body contamination can be minimized by using vegetative buffers alongside waterways, terracing and contour farming as erosion control techniques, and using fertilizers and pesticides responsibly.

Moreover, duck farming enterprises can lessen their carbon footprint by integrating renewable energy sources like solar or wind power. Farmers can help create a more sustainable energy environment and reduce greenhouse gas emissions by utilizing clean energy. A more resilient and ecologically friendly duck farming system can result from the implementation of these waste management and environmental impact reduction measures.

USING ENVIRONMENTALLY FRIENDLY SOLUTIONS IN OPERATIONS

It is crucial to include environmentally friendly solutions into regular operations if duck farming is to become more sustainable. This involves implementing integrated pest management (IPM) techniques to reduce the need for pesticides and manage pests using organic methods such as crop rotation, habitat modification, and biological control agents. IPM supports wildlife and beneficial insects on farms, which not only lessens the impact on the environment but also increases biodiversity.

Moreover, lowering operating expenses and environmental impact can be achieved by putting into practice efficient energy and resource usage techniques. The sustainability of duck farming operations can be greatly increased by utilizing energy-efficient equipment, maximizing water consumption with drip irrigation and water recycling systems, and lowering waste generation with recycling and reuse programs. An agricultural paradigm that is more robust and environmentally conscientious may result from using these eco-friendly alternatives.

Furthermore, implementing sustainable sourcing methods such as buying locally produced commodities, endorsing fair labor standards, and supporting organic and regenerative agriculture can enhance community resilience and establish a more sustainable supply chain. Duck farmers can positively benefit society, the environment, and their financial results by giving eco-friendly solutions priority in their operations.

ENCOURAGEMENT OF BIODIVERSITY AND NATURAL ENVIRONMENTS

Sustainable duck farming methods must prioritize protecting natural habitats and promoting biodiversity. By giving a variety of species somewhere to live, eat, and build their nests, duck farms can contribute to biodiversity by creating wildlife-friendly environments.

By establishing hedgerows, planting native plants, and protecting wetlands and water bodies, one might draw beneficial wildlife, such as amphibians, pollinators, and pest predators, and so support the balance of the environment.

Incorporating agroecological concepts into farming practices, such as crop diversification, polyculture, and mixed farming systems, can also improve biodiversity and ecological resilience. By imitating natural ecosystems, these techniques improve soil health, lessen dependency on chemical inputs, and support a variety of plant and animal species.

Additionally, you may help conserve species and protect habitat by taking part in conservation programs, funding habitat restoration projects, and working with regional conservation organizations. Duck farmers can build a more resilient and sustainable farming environment that promotes wildlife and agricultural productivity by actively promoting biodiversity and natural habitats.

ASSESSING THE LONG-TERM VIABILITY OF DUCKLING PRODUCTION

Duckling farming's long-term viability and resilience are ensured by evaluating the industry's effects on the environment, the economy, and society. To increase sustainability performance, frequent sustainability audits and evaluations can point out areas for development and serve as a roadmap for strategic decision-making.

Resilience to environmental disruptions and climate change is one facet of long-term sustainability. Resilience to climate variability and extreme weather events can be increased by putting climate-smart strategies into effect, such as water-efficient irrigation, conservation of soil, and drought-resistant agricultural types. This will ensure continuous productivity and stability.

Long-term sustainability also depends on fostering social justice and economic viability in duck farming communities.

A more resilient and inclusive agriculture sector can be achieved by promoting fair labor practices, funding farmer education and training, and encouraging community development.

Additionally, ongoing innovation, study, and adaptation to new opportunities and challenges can improve duckling farming's long-term viability. Duck farmers may position themselves for success in a rapidly changing agricultural landscape by embracing technological improvements, investigating alternate production methods, and remaining educated about market trends and consumer preferences.

Duckling farmers have the opportunity to establish a robust and sustainable agricultural system that will benefit the environment, society, and economy for future generations by assessing and addressing these critical elements of long-term sustainability.

CHAPTER ELEVEN

UPCOMING DEVELOPMENTS AND TRENDS

EXAMINING TECHNOLOGICAL DEVELOPMENTS IN DUCKLING PRODUCTION

The world of duckling farming has seen incredible technological breakthroughs in recent years, completely changing the nuances of duck breeding, raising, and management. Automated feeding systems, which employ sensors and algorithms to precisely monitor and administer feed depending on the nutritional demands of the ducks, are one important area of innovation. This lowers labor costs and feeds waste while also guaranteeing optimal growth and health.

The application of machine learning and artificial intelligence (AI) to duckling farming is another noteworthy advancement. To maximize farm management choices, AI-powered systems can evaluate enormous volumes of data about duck behavior, health indicators, and environmental aspects. AI systems, for instance, can automate some operations, like collecting eggs, and even forecast disease outbreaks and breeding cycles.

Furthermore, advances in genetic engineering have resulted in the creation of breeds with superior features like increased feed conversion efficiency, disease resistance, and faster growth rates. These genetically engineered ducks help farmers increase their output and profits while satisfying the market's rising demand for premium duck products. All things considered, the business is changing as a result of these technical developments in duckling farming, which increase farmer profitability, sustainability, and efficiency.

TRENDS IN MARKET DEMAND AND CONSUMER PREFERENCES

Market demands and consumer tastes are major factors in determining how duckling growers formulate their strategies. The growing desire from consumers for duck goods that are produced responsibly and with ethical practices is one notable development. Ducks raised in natural settings with access to clean water, open areas, and a natural diet are the focus of free-range and organic duck farming methods, which have become more popular as a result.

The increasing demand for specialty duck items, like duck eggs, duck meat cuts, and gourmet duck treats, is another trend. Demand for distinctive and superior duck products is being driven by consumers' growing inclination toward more daring culinary selections. Duckling producers can take advantage of this trend to expand their product lines and target certain consumer groups.

Additionally, customers are becoming more conscious of the health advantages of duck products, especially because they are a lean protein source and a good source of important nutrients.

There are now opportunities to sell duck products as a tasty and nutritious substitute for other meats thanks to this health-conscious trend. By matching their production methods and marketing approaches to customer preferences and market demands, duckling farmers can profit from these changes.

PROSPECTS FOR GROWTH AND DIVERSIFICATION

There are lots of chances for growth and diversification in the changing duckling farming scene. Value-added processing, which turns duck ingredients into gourmet dinners, ready-to-cook meals, or specialized goods like duck confit and pâté, is one important area of opportunity. Value-added processing creates new markets and revenue sources for farmers in addition to adding value to duck products.

There is also a chance in global markets, where there is an increasing need for premium duck goods, particularly in areas where duck is a main ingredient in culinary traditions. Farmers may find that exporting duck goods is a profitable way to grow their consumer base and boost revenue. Nonetheless, it necessitates adherence to quality standards and international trade laws.

Moreover, expanding into allied industries like farm-to-table dining, duck-themed attractions, or agritourism can boost the overall sustainability of duckling farming operations and offer new revenue streams. Duckling farmers can attain development, resilience, and sustained success in a competitive market by recognizing and seizing these chances.

CHANGING INDUSTRY AND REGULATORY STANDARDS AND HOW TO ADJUST

Farmers must constantly adapt to and comply with changing industry standards and regulatory requirements related to the duckling farming business. Animal welfare requirements are one area of concentration; these laws cover things like housing conditions, outdoor space access, and humane treatment methods.

Farmers are required to maintain compliance with rules while staying up to date on these standards and taking appropriate action to guarantee the welfare of their ducks.

Food safety and traceability are also crucial, requiring strict certifications and standards to ensure the consumer's safety and satisfaction with duck products. To satisfy legal requirements and consumer expectations, farmers must employ strong food safety standards, traceability systems, and quality assurance methods across the production and supply chain.

Furthermore, rules and norms aiming at lowering environmental consequences including waste management, greenhouse gas emissions, and water pollution are making environmental sustainability in duckling farming a priority. To comply with rules and support environmental conservation efforts, farmers are encouraged to use sustainable farming techniques, apply resource-efficient technologies, and participate in eco-friendly projects.

TECHNIQUES FOR MAINTAINING INNOVATION AND COMPETITION IN THE MARKET

Duckling farmers must use smart methods in a cutthroat market to remain inventive and competitive.

To set themselves apart from rivals and draw highly discerning customers, farmers might use differentiation through branding and marketing, emphasizing distinctive selling factors like organic farming, heritage breeds, or specialty goods.

Utilizing technology and data analytics to optimize farm operations, boost productivity, and cut expenses is another tactic. To increase output and profitability, this entails putting in place data-driven decision-making procedures, IoT-enabled monitoring systems, and precision farming techniques.

Furthermore, cooperation and joint ventures among food manufacturers, distributors, and retailers can boost market penetration, optimize distribution networks, and generate synergies. Duckling farmers may boost their competitiveness in the business, gain access to new markets, and grow their market share by forming strategic alliances and integrating their value chain.

Continuous innovation can also help brands stand out from the competition, identify market trends, and increase consumer loyalty through improvements in product development, packaging, and customer experience. Duckling farmers may prosper in a changing and competitive market environment by remaining flexible, sensitive, and agile in response to consumer tastes and market dynamics.

www.ingramcontent.com/pod-product-compliance
Lightning Source LLC
Chambersburg PA
CBHW071837210526
45479CB00001B/184